SING & HIDE

Cai Draper is a writer from South London, living in Norwich. In 2018 he completed an MA in Creative Writing (Poetry) at UEA. His first pamphlet, *SPRUNG*, was published by Broken Sleep Books. Other work, including flash and non-fiction, has been published in various journals, magazines and anthologies. He organises and hosts poetry events and workshops, collaborating regularly with the Book Hive, the National Centre for Writing and other organisations. More information and a selection of writing can be found at www.caidraper.com.

sing & hide

Published by Bad Betty Press in 2022
www.badbettypress.com

Cover image of *London Pride* by Frank Dobson (1951)
used and adapted with permission from the Goldmark Gallery

Printed and bound in the United Kingdom

A CIP record of this book is available from the British Library.

ISBN: 978-1-913268-35-0

sing & hide

For my family

Contents

Single Form

after Barbara Hepworth

The sculpture is of me. A monolith
of London turf. Blue, green, dun
gold teetering. And this curiosity:
its main feature is perfect
circular space
where metal was. The words
I've flung through there: fear,
shame, rage, taking flight in the
rank expression of language.
If you know the secret to why we sing
and hide our faces, I am listening.

Mummies Love Me Mummy Mum Mother Present Family

found on etsy.com

Gay family doll family. Small woven
canvas family. Christmas tree
decoration sleigh 3, 4, 5 family.
Toddler pride t-shirt family.
Rainbow striped moccasin family.
Mummies love me baby
blue embroidered motto family.
Gears and cogs family. Love is love
family. Mummy mummy me
special pillow case family.
Pebble heart family. Wedding art family.
Gender neutral which parent
trivia game family. Mrs & Mrs
bodysuit family. Seriously dad
gift card family. DNA is overrated
funny onesie family.

FODs & Son

1.

Yeah lesbians raised me in Elephant and Castle.
So many maybe I'm
not a lesbian but almost everyone
else is. Scores of so-called aunties
on motorbikes book groups
ballroom dancing at the Rivoli.
They call themselves the FODs.
The Fat Old Dykes.

Mum has longer hair than some. I pretend
she's normal at parents' evening.
Pride is embarrassing. Camping with a friend
who goes *My mum and your mum like women*
innit. This one in the tent so naïve.
What's the first rule of lesbian mum club?
I'm on the phone to god –
Where the hell's my dad? Read men and weep
I'd like to be called Mark from now on please.
Mark my inner Clark Kent in a phone box.

No Mark no Superman but
Mum Suse Fran Jules Jane Chris
Fiona Jude Jackie Joy Anna Darryl Bev.
I'm on the phone to heaven, going
Where's my fanny? Why am I the only one
with a willy in this family?

2.

Then I went to college
and said, 'My mum's gay.'
And they said, 'Cool!'
And I said, 'Yes. Cool.'
And my sister said, 'Yeah, it's cool.'
And to myself I said, 'Cool. *Cool.*'
And they said, 'So…?!'
And I said, 'Turkey baster.'
And they looked at each other, and they looked at me
and said, 'Tell us *everything*.'

In Youngness

how we ever in youngness grazed on the day
scabbed up & matchstick
knees about gravel
splayed red in the passages

my friend your house
a slow train of safety swum from

the world aimless & Friday
and I would say TV those days
was the extra wine your mum could savour

yeah I remember tipping the living room door ajar

her on all fours in underwear growling

how swift the stairs recalled me

but as for swimming at Peckham Pulse

the pubic hair you showed me in the changing room was on its ones

quivering shrapnel in the fountain

& always chips under ketchup

you

very Fresh Prince

me so Aquila

haul / between

In memory of Martin Draper & Neville Lucas

I was scared to make this poem /
treat them right / they never
came close to meeting in life so
how to present them dead /
I'd have them here retold as bodiless
friends with shears / with god /
dear ghosts / may you bring these
families together in death /
may your souls fold up the long haul
between us / here is the pen in my breast
tearing space

Portrait from Memory

swag   chuckle   blue jean for a Megadrive

cream smooth garment   living room sweet boy

say the telly is deep as broad cousin

Sonic getting coin on a Saturday

now this   how nineties   say no one is too good for you

the way he ties my Gooner scarf pristine   level up

two step ridden like a wave   I can't

I'm begging him to turn it down

I'm eight   his name is hidden

in a crowd   in a zone

never get caught with a knife cousin

on sofa French kissing   I witness   say pulling   I can't

Moschino ads line the walls like art

arch perfection of the Bulls cap

he's all caught up in the crush   level up

pub   noughties   say hear me I'd die for you

my shirt in his fist   but I can't

in Spoons   both listen and fight

his texts from the suburb in the morning

In the Queue at Woolworths

as we are now with mum and the buying, and the not buying of things, and the never-ending spaghetti junction of her feelings about that moment at the counter in Elephant & Castle Woolworths, when I tugged on the reluctant trouser leg of her, like, please can I have the toy sheriff set with star, handcuff and cap gun, the actual plastic dream of it, she must have thought, no way, while knowing it was a bright Saturday, could be outside getting sun on our cheeks and I've got my boy queuing in Woolworths with no say at all, so she said, fine, go and get the toy sheriff set, and I was all yesss, and full of words on it, and she was glad for making me happy, but because joy was tainted by guilt for the mass of packaging, and the fact that you don't buy your kid stuff just because they ask for it, and the short-lived significance of the four ninety-nine, and knowing the violence of police invades young minds, she decided it was time for a compromise, and I knew somehow not to look too shocked or upset when we opened the toy sheriff set on the concourse outside and threw the cap gun in the bin.

Ecotone

The leather-bound matter of
my father's back in the water
is all in view. The deal maker
whose own family holds me
in the ecotone with Dad
on the tip of my tongue.
So Greg is the name of the man
who rolls through the waves
I watch from shallows.
His thick unflinching front crawl
shifts my spine. I must follow.

Pa

Does he like crumpet butter on his 'tache?
Did the squib of my sad chatter come from upstairs, or down,
or the chairs, or the pasta, or the speakers, near,
or far?

Does he find it easy as it looks?
Does he jump across the boulders as an ibex, or a goat,
or a bighorn, or a mouflon,
or a chamois?

Is the devil in his detail?
Does he keep his hearing aids in a case, or an intricate box,
or a small velvet bag with a drawstring,
or a jar?

Does he pretend he doesn't pray?
At Sainsbury's does he say much obliged, or 'preciate it,
or thank you, or thanks, or cheers,
or ta?

Why didn't he come to graduation?
Does he like his feats of nature deep, or erotic,
or bioluminescent, or quiet, or epic,
or bizarre?

Was he harried by a bully in after school club?
Would the melody of his anthem be played on synth brass, or Theremin,
or sound box under bald spot, or heartstrings, or waves,
or guitar?

Did he mean to teach his daughter the art of warfare?
Does he daydream I die gracelessly by Segway, or submarine,
or helicopter, or hot air balloon, or dinghy, or crane,
or car?

Does he sniff his fingers after picking at his toenails?
How self-conscious does he feel when he enters a raffle, or a traffic jam,
or a lobby, or information, or a chamber, or a country,
or a bar?

Was he glad when I was born?
Has he ever fucked off with a fire chief, or a philanderer,
or an Ofsted inspector, or a sylph, or a nightmare, or a gasman,
or a czar?

Does he know what some men are?
Has he ever had trouble with an engine, or a substance,
or a friend, or the law, or depressive episodes,
or a bra?

Was it easy to keep me a secret from his family?
Does he know what I mean when I say gun, or cuss,
or rinse, or boy,
or par?

Extra Terrestrial

happy joyously yes I film the dead
kangaroo on my iPad flies rise
like birds to flock
return to Aus

the
out
back

guts on the dust road 'must
have been a truck' you don't say scrub
peels away gumbark to horizon *look!* the scoffing
we hear when our
guide says
her people are from the dream time

Australia in general Baz Luhrmann

Aussie or not I show off a lot
but I'm scared of the
sea it's too deep and
BEWARE OF THE SHARKS spiders things
that jump
quickly the main thing
I worry about is not genocidal racism
fatal bugs or the beach body but
the way
the belly goes

when my father his partner and daughter do their

<MOVING-TOGETHER-AS-A-UNIT>
thing

I'm in the same nation but

1800pt

after Fiona Banner

It's hard to believe
they are, perhaps, without
language. A full stop
(I didn't know what that was
exactly): a pause or end,
a breath in between. The people
might be the letters. Becoming real.
Solidifying. Like a sentence
from which the words have been removed, these
things have just popped out from fiction.
They made my father realise
how beautiful the trees are.

Three Standing Figures

after Henry Moore

a pervading
sense of
communion

overlay

release

chiselled

conscious
of the air

with a lifted
gaze
for
distances

Velvet Imaginary

These days in a walking cloud you are getting to me
with those massive thoughts you grow through the trunk
of yourself in America
you only get bigger as bigger as the news
on my air on the daily I wonder
how you do all this living on me
when all your being away has turned me into a toy
I barely can see myself in the mirror
I look in the mirror a lot and wonder
if I've ever really known anyone including myself
but the ways you show me
I do are bounteous.

The solitude of pain & coming listing the only way
[no conjugation, etc.] I come
back to me at home I smoke
all the weed alone I hear the neighbours learn
the piano.

My sisters are telling me they're pregnant.

I want to go cycling. It is good
for the environment. When each one told me
I acted different. I love them uniquely
the same. As in family. As in bloody
adults. As in dead whales. Change occurs
in other heads only. I want to buy equipment.
I go along with it all as in jokes as in where to shop
to save the planet. Too many things are happening.
I try to explain the fam to Lotte. I jockey
for precision. My sisters are telling me
they're pregnant. I have a hundred unread books.
A line of poetry: *the environment exists*
in the VIP suite of white inquiry. I've gone dairy free
except for butter, milk & yoghurt. Everyday storms,
everyday fortress, everyday Sports Direct.
England tempts me as a notion. The rain today jars
like a bad definition. #worldcupofbread is in my dreams.
Jeff Bezos is in my dreams. Frightened cyclops pigs are
in my dreams. My sisters are telling me they're pregnant.
The receptionist is excited about using Telegram. People get away
with fiction. Everyday displacement, everyday
pickets, everyday extinction. Extinction rebellion
was banned from the dinner table. It didn't last two minutes.
My sisters are telling me they're pregnant. Their babies
will inherit their skin. Lots of my friends
hate XR except Nathan *those middle class wankers*
are doing an exceptional job and my mum

they are not the enemy. The world turns
burning. I am considering
many options. Everyday acidification, everyday state
aggression, everyday billions of edible bananas
in the bin. Floods, foodbanks,
rigor mortis muntjac on the A11.
Mirror neurons, nicotine pangs, the neighbour's banging
on the wall when we bang, the vilification of Drill,
the cloud, the spying, the ground, the sky,
the doorway. Everything is not
fine. My sisters are telling me they're pregnant.
Everyone's talking about everything
all the time. I send photos
of the scans
to the group.

London Pride

after Frank Dobson

They are thinking and as strong as ever –
my mother and her lover cast in bronze.
Less phoenix from the blitz rubble
more Mum's true material.
Me and my sis duck out and weave
about South Bank's playground sculpture
and gather ourselves to explain
our very conception to near strangers.
Yes, we've met our fathers.
No, we're not test tube babies.
Each New Year's Eve we clung onto
Mum's failing knees, clutching glowsticks
fireworks burst the river. Clear,
our legs are surer by the current
of the Thames lit to bloom like a family.

NR3 X SE5

ever since the muscles in the sky
did their thing & we got burgled
I've been craving specific winds
of hot market phone stations
& shouting shops South East
where places meet   I'm taken
to imbibing delightful concrete scapes
my mother galloping
into her own hegemony/benevolence
                                        beyond the fields of these limits
in Broadland saturation I see
sky   flat water   shining
like the sky   it cups a light
& here gleams a silvery world
in ever-morphosis
the mice vacating my gaff in wee
& meek hours I find myself
in need of inflatable
computer game figures from the 80s
done with discipline & a tropical
Yarmouth panache
                    in Camberwell
back when there were locks
on the gates of the Green

I wonder if the shops had queues
of desperate swimmers hankering
for pies not falafel

still

when a broad ridge of starlight
hits Burgess Park barbecue fiesta smoke
& swaying tree season
when it's Frisbee time
when that dude on his mountain bike
came on to us & you said
I'm not about that life
which I thought was a bit homophobic
even though I felt weirder
afterwards on the stoop we saw
he'd found his man maybe beside the lake
they film so much by

where's the parts for us anyhow

the trickledown a soundbite
that isn't trickling down to any
public water feature round these parts

still

they are some of the best
water features of my life

Author's Note

It would be fitting to stay silent,
like bronze figures or stone
under moss. My mum was gay on the quiet.

To get it accurate, I convey the shame
when my best friend said,
they're lesbians but they're alright.

I cast Mum and Jules in *London Pride.*
I plagiarise and stoop to plinths.
Feel what meanings fit.

Notes

‘Single Form’: Barbara’s Hepworth’s sculpture *Single Form (BH 314)* stands in Battersea Park.

‘Mummies Love Me…’: The entirety of the text in this poem is lifted from items listed on etsy.com which appeared when I put ‘gay parent family’ into the site’s search bar.

‘FODs and Son’: I was not actually conceived with a turkey baster.

‘Three Standing Figures’: Most of the text from this poem was found in an interview with Henry Moore, source lost.

‘Pa’: I wrote this poem after reading ‘The Akond of Swat’ by Edward Lear.

‘1800pt’: Fiona Banner’s sculptures *Full Stop* are located outside City Hall, London. The text from this poem was lifted from an interview with Fiona Banner which can be found here: http://www.fionabanner.com/words/makingitreal.htm

‘My sisters are telling me they’re pregnant’: ‘Where to shop to save the planet’ was a headline from the *Eastern Daily Press* on 16th July 2019. Babies Ines and Orla were born healthy in 2020.

Acknowledgements

Thanks to the editors of the following magazines for giving some of these poems a first home: *Poet's Directory*, *LESLIE* magazine, *Poetical*, *Porridge* magazine, *bath magg*, *Lighthouse* journal, *Unlost* journal, *Tentacular* magazine and the *Ekphrastic Review*.

Huge love, gratitude and respect to all my family, especially my mum, Lucy Draper.

Special thanks to Gboyega and Ellen.

Lightning Source UK Ltd.
Milton Keynes UK
UKHW011832270223
417744UK00001B/4